ORSAY

visitor's guide

Françoise Bayle

art lys :

Cover: Vincent van Gogh, *Portrait of the Artist*, detail
and Pierre-Auguste Renoir, *Dancing at the Moulin de la Galette, Montmartre*, detail
Page 3: Vincent van Gogh, *Starry Night*, detail
Pages 4 and 5: central aisle of the musée d'Orsay

Editorial co-ordination: Denis Kilian
Graphic design: Martine Mène
Plans: Thierry Lebreton, Dominique Bissière
Editorial and iconographic follow-up: Karine Barou and Hervé Delemotte
Production: Pierre Kegels

Warning:
Owing the extensions currently being carried out in the museum, it is possible that works may be moved or not be on view.

ISBN: 2-85495-199-9
© ARTLYS, Versailles, 2002

Contents

View of a terrace, Seine side and rue de Lille side, on the middle floor

GROUND FLOOR

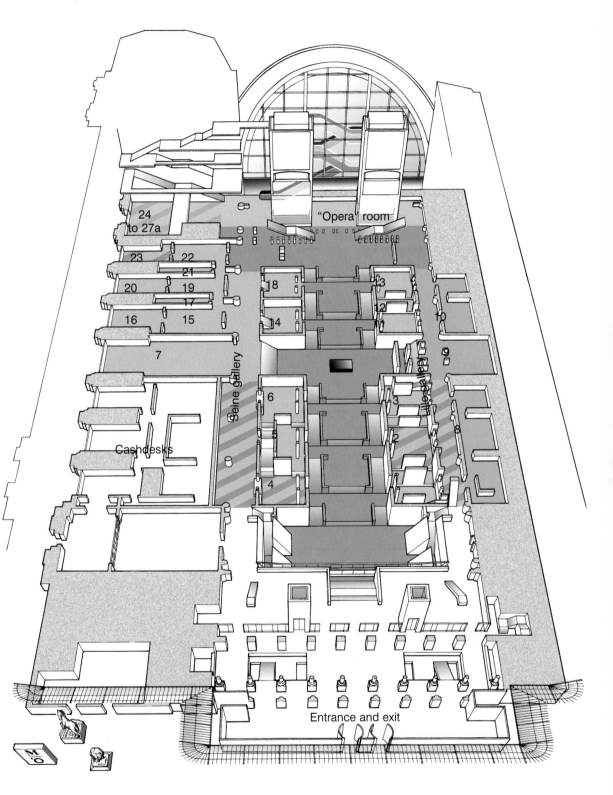

During the works to extend the temporary exhibition rooms, the shop is,
for the time being, situated in Rooms 19 and 20.
The works are divided between numbered rooms. They are sometimes moved
around or removed according to the loans agreed for an exhibition.

TOP FLOOR

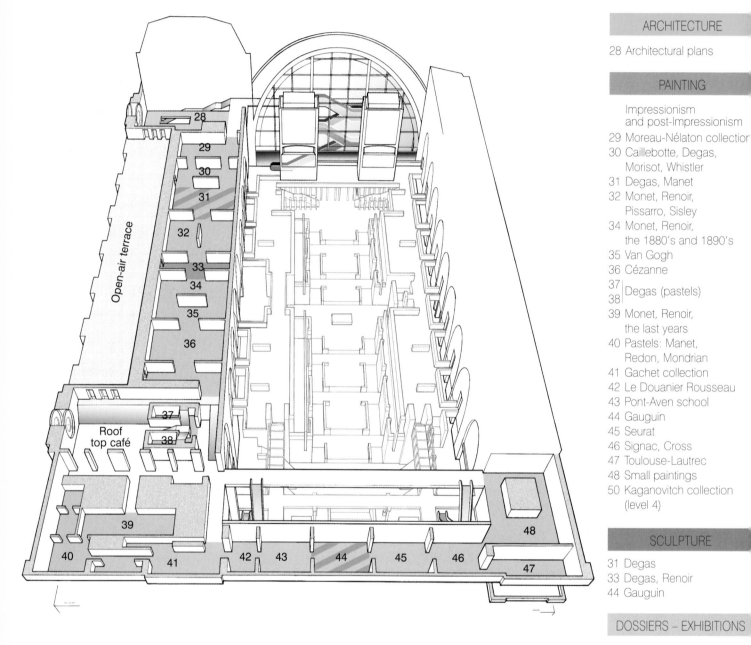

28

29

30

31

32

33

34

35

36

Open-air terrace

37

38

Roof top café

39

40

41

42 43 44 45 46

48

47

MIDDLE LEVEL

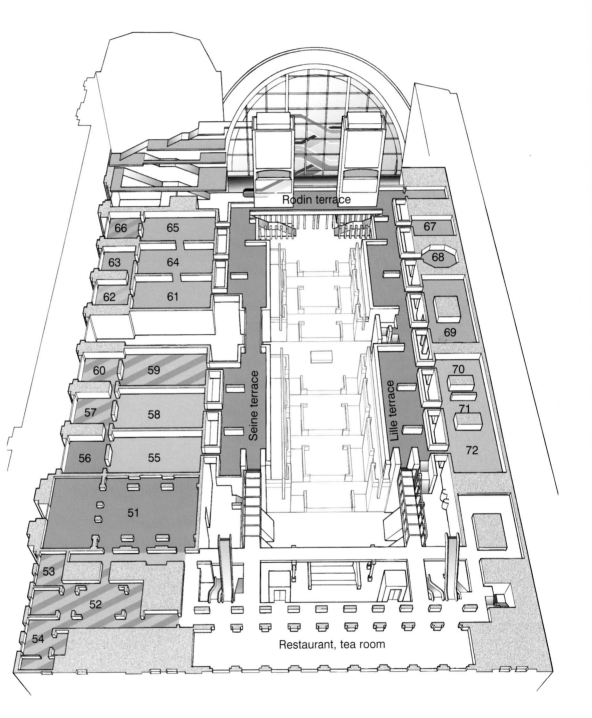

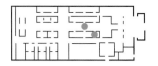

1. JEAN-BAPTISTE, know as AUGUSTE CLESINGER, *Woman Bitten by a Serpent*, 1847, marble, 56.5 x 180 cm, Salon of 1847
2. HONORÉ DAUMIER, *Laurent Cunin*, one of the *Celebrities of the 'Juste Milieu'*, 1831, unbaked clay coloured with oil, 15 x 13 cm
3. FRANÇOIS RUDE, *The Genius of the Motherland*, 1836, cast taken in 1898 from the relief of the Arc de l'Étoile, plaster, 224 x 196 cm
4. ANTOINE-LOUIS BARYE, *Lion Sitting*, 1847, patinated plaster, 200 x 186 cm

These works are situated on the ground floor, in the central aisle and in Room 4.

Sculpture pre-1850

Daumier modelled busts, "clay snapshots", of great psychological intensity in order to produce, for *La Caricature*, a series of portraits of politicians of the July monarchy, a government of the "very centre equally distant from the excesses of popular power and the abuses of royal power".

The lascivious nudity of the model was not the only reason for the scandal that would be provoked by the exhibition of this sculpture, Clesinger's first success. The critics in fact accused him, probably justifiably, of having worked from a cast taken of the body of Apollonie Sabatier – the folds of cellulite were enough to convince of it. Scandalous in the eyes of prudish society, on Sundays she gathered together some of the most famous artistic personalities of the time: Goncourt, Delacroix, Préault, Flaubert, Gautier, Baudelaire and others – she was, moreover, the mistress of these last two.

2

All the romanticism of Rude is expressed in this head with its strong contrasts of light and shade: the allegory of the Motherland with its bulging eyes, screaming mouth and dented forehead. Having got his wife to pose, it is said that he continually urged her to yell louder...

3

4

More placid that most of the spiritedly-clashing wild beasts that were usually sculpted by the "Michelangelo of the Menagerie", this *Lion Sitting* is, however, very true to life: just like Delacroix, Barye regularly went to observe the animals in the zoos of the period. "Nature then! Nature and Truth", declared Victor Hugo in his preface to *Cromwell*, a true manifesto of Romanticism.

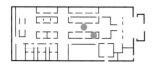

1. JEAN-BAPTISTE CARPEAUX, *Eugénie Fiocre*, 1869, plaster, 83 x 51 cm
2. JEAN-BAPTISTE CARPEAUX, *Ugolin*, 1862, bronze, 194 x 148 cm
3. JEAN-BAPTISTE CARPEAUX, *The Prince Imperial and his Dog Nero*, 1865, marble, 140 x 65 cm
4. JEAN-BAPTISTE CARPEAUX, *The Dance,* commissioned by Charles Garnier to decorate the façade of the Opera, 1865-1869, stone, 420 x 298 cm; a replica now stands at the Paris Opera

These works are situated on the ground floor, in the central aisle.

Jean-Baptiste Carpeaux

Carpeaux also executed a great many expressive, lifelike busts which achieved enormous success, such as that of the prima ballerina Eugénie Fiocre, an "impish show-off in her pretty slenderness", as the Goncourts had described her.

1

3

Professor of drawing and sculpture to the prince, Carpeaux was soon commissioned to produce portraits of several members of the imperial family. He was immensely successful: everyone praised their likeness and simplicity - the prince is shown in his usual clothes. Commissions came flooding in: in bronze, marble and bisque.

The subject, taken from Dante's *Inferno*, recounts a passage in the story of Ugolino della Gherardesca, the 13th century tyrant of Pisa, shut up with his children by his rival until they died. "When I recognised my own appearance on those four faces, I bit my hands with sorrow, and my children, thinking that it was hunger, suddenly got up and said, "Oh, father! It would hurt us less if you ate us"."

2

When the four groups intended to decorate the façade of the new Opera were unveiled on 27th July 1869, Carpeaux's attracted all the criticism: if he "contrasts boldly with the noble style, content, of the compositions which surround him", he also enrages the prim and proper minds which talked of Maenads that "smell of vice and reek of wine". To such an extent that on the night of 27th to 28th August, a bottle of ink was thrown at the sculpture. The pressure was so strong that Napoleon III decided to have the group removed: a new commission was given to the sculptor Gumery, who began working on a more chaste group when the '70 war broke out. *The Dance* would remain in place.

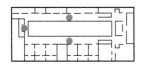

These works are situated on the middle floor, the terraces and the top floor, in Room 31.

Sculpture post-1880

1

This *Dancer* is the only sculpture which Degas in fact wanted to exhibit in his lifetime, although he produced many others. Moreover, the original, in coloured wax with the hair tied back with a satin ribbon and dressed in authentic clothes, caused a lively reaction, probably due to its uncompromising realism. "The terrible reality of this statuette produces… a clear sense of unease", wrote Huysmans who, nevertheless, defended the work.

Commissioned by the State in 1880, *The Gate of Hell* would haunt the sculptor to the end of his days. In order to illustrate the torments of hell evoked by Dante's *Divine Comedy,* he gradually moves towards a décor rich in detail for which he modelled countless pieces which often became independent works. His figures, where the hollows and projections create strong contrasts of light and shade, bear witness to the formidable strength of expression which Rodin conferred on his sculpted bodies throughout his life: "The body," he said, "is a cast on which the passions are imprinted."

2

Compared with Rodin, who sought expression above all, Maillol seemed in particular to want to express self-control and equilibrium. Whereas the former multiplied viewpoints and outlines to give the impression of a body with bones, muscles and flesh, Maillol's single viewpoint, the simplification of forms and smooth treatment of the medium lead to a feeling of harmony and accepted gravity.

3

A number of Camille Claudel's sculptures relate the various periods in her liaison with Rodin. In a large oblique composition, *Maturity* shows Camille, on her knees and pleading, holding her hands out to Rodin who has already left her. "What lends unique interest to my sister's work is that, all the way through, it is the story of her life, her remnants...", wrote Paul Claudel, the artist's brother.

4

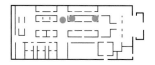

1. ALEXANDRE CABANEL, *The Birth of Venus*, 1863, oil on canvas, 130 x 225 cm, Salon of 1863
2. THOMAS COUTURE, *Romans of the Decadence*, 1847, oil on canvas, 472 x 772 cm, Salon of 1847
3. JEAN AUGUSTE DOMINIQUE INGRES, *Spring*, 1820-1856, oil on canvas, 163 x 80 cm

These works are situated on the ground floor, in the central aisle and in Rooms 1 and 3.

Classicism and Eclecticism

Shown at the same Salon as Manet's *The Picnic* which itself caused a scandal, this canvas achieved great success – it was immediately bought by the Emperor. "The flesh is ideal and divine", wrote Théophile Gautier. A magnificent example of the official taste of the Second Empire, this nude, in the aesthetic tradition of Ingres, is shown in a completely unreal seascape and improbable colours. Here, mythology is used as a justification, for ultimately, an erotic scene: the lascivious pose and gaze of Venus are, to say the least, eloquent.

The subject of immense success, this canvas fully met the criteria for historical art, which continued to prevail in the hierarchy of the genres: very large format, use of the golden section, subject drawn from ancient literature, clear geometric composition, use of perspective. Moreover, in borrowing from the masters of the past – Antiquity, Venetian painting, the art of Raphael –, Couture is a perfect representative of the Eclecticism which still held sway in France at that time.

Compared with the Romantic Delacroix, Ingres embodied, until the 1850's, the other major pictorial trend, Classicism. The feminine allegory depicting the source and coming straight out of Antiquity was the pretext for the artist to paint a nude, a theme which punctuates all his work and remained a much favoured subject for the Academic painters who were the heirs of the Neo-Classicism of David, Ingres's teacher. As often, the latter attempted to reconcile imitation of nature and the fine ideal: "There is nothing of essence to be found in art after Pheidias and Raphael, but, even after them, there are still things that need to be done to maintain the cult of Truth and perpetuate the tradition of the Beautiful."

3

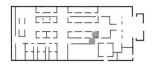

1. HONORÉ DAUMIER, *Don Quixote and the Dead Mule*, 1867, oil on canvas, 132.5 x 54.5 cm
2. ROSA BONHEUR, *Ploughing in the Nivernais Region: First Dressing*, 1849, oil on canvas, 134 x 260 cm, Salon of 1849
3. HONORÉ DAUMIER, *The Laundress*, circa 1863, oil on wood, 49 x 33.5 cm

These works are situated on the ground floor, in the Seine Gallery and in Room 4.

A certain realism

1

Painted to decorate the hall of Daubigny's house at Auvers-sur-Oise, this canvas illustrates a passage from Cervantes's *Don Quijote*, a novel which inspired several of Daumier's works. Here, the rapid brush, with little colour on it, stylised the two silhouettes, one light and slender, the other squat and dark, who stumble upon the body of the mule, simply outlined.

After a long career doing drawings and as a caricaturist in anti-establishment newspapers, which earned him several months in prison under the July Monarchy, Daumier came to sculpture then to painting. He was then some forty years old, and despite the admiration of a number of artists and critics – Balzac, Baudelaire, Michelet or Delacroix –, he remained in his own time underestimated as a painter. In his realistic canvases where the areas of light and shade are often contrasted, he endeavoured above all to represent his town-dwelling contemporaries – landscapes did not interest him –, often taking up the same themes: lawyers, train travellers, acrobats, laundresses and the like. These two anonymous figures, simply sketched, nevertheless express all the fatigue of a day's labour. "The idea emerges straightaway, you look, you've understood": this comment by Baudelaire, which was applied to Daumier's satirical cartoons, also went for his paintings. The theme of the laundress, then a very modern one, would soon be taken up by other artists such as Degas and Toulouse-Lautrec.

3

The realism of Rosa Bonheur, which has sometimes paradoxically been called academic realism, is different. This daughter of an artist, much patronised by the imperial court, began a brilliant career at an early age, in which official duties – she was director of the *École impériale de dessin* – did not prevent her from being appreciated as far away as England and the United States.

2

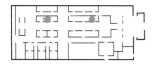

1. EUGÈNE DELACROIX, *The Lion Hunt*, sketch from 1854, oil on canvas, 86 x 115 cm
2. THÉODORE CHASSÉRIAU, " *Tepidarium*", a room where the women of Pompeii came to relax and dry themselves after bathing, 1853, oil on canvas, 171 x 258 cm, Salon of 1853
3. GUSTAVE MOREAU, *Orpheus*, 1865, oil on wood, 154 x 99.5 cm, Salon of 1866

These works are situated on the ground floor, in Rooms 2 and 12.

Romantics and Symbolists

In this great sketch, Delacroix fell within the tradition of Rubens in terms of both theme and technique. For the leader of the Romantics, the composition of space and forms was achieved through colour and not through line, as with Ingres, an ardent defender of Neo-Classicism. The very expression of movement and emotion, the outlines do not subdue the colour. In comparison with the coldness and stiffness of the Neo-Classicists, the Romantics in this way reinstated colour paints and pictorial technique.

1

A pupil of Ingres, but also very attracted by the painting of Delacroix, Chassériau worked actively for compromise: whilst the sinuous lines still define female bodies, as with Ingres, the method of applying colour, sometimes pure, is closer to the art of the Delacroix. As for classical inspiration, this was more to be sought in the trip he made to Italy at the beginning of the 1840's and during which he visited, amongst other places, Naples and Pompeii, where public baths had been modernised. But Antiquity, as often at the time, was a pretext for an orientalised, languid scene which, really, owed as much to Ingres as to Delacroix.

20

2

few years later, Moreau fell within
e tradition of Delacroix and
hassériau, whom he admired.
s taste for heroes straight out
Greek and Eastern mythology,
s imagination quick to create
elancholic, mysterious worlds,
s attraction for the bizarrely,
ghtly morbid, beautiful, his
jection of art which contented
elf with the appearance of
ngs make him possibly the last
the Romantics and one of the
st Symbolists.

3

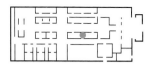

1. THÉODORE ROUSSEAU, *An Avenue, Forest on Adam's Island*, 1846-1849, oil on canvas, 101 x 82 cm, Salon of 1849
2. CAMILLE COROT, *Dance of the Nymphs*, 1860-1865, oil on canvas, 47 x 77.5 cm
3. JEAN-FRANÇOIS MILLET, *The Angelus*, 1857-1859, oil on canvas, 55.5 x 66 cm

These works are situated on the ground floor, in Room 5.

All these painters frequented Barbizon

It was at the house of Father Ganne, an art lover, that the painters of the "Barbizon School" gathered in this small village on the outskirts of the Forest of Fontainebleau. After Corot and Huet, Rousseau, Dupré, Troyon, Daubigny and Millet painted here, from life, studies which they then re-worked in the studio, often using heavy, thick paint.

Corot's style developed from the 1850's: his landscapes were now bathed in a slightly misty atmosphere which gave them a more lyrical tonality. Inspired both by the rough drawings he had done in Italy and the sketches he made when he went to the Opera, here, *Dance of the Nymphs*, a recomposed landscape, is one of the various versions he would produce on this theme using a light, vibrant stroke. An unclassifiable artist, whilst Corot, through the sobriety of his compositions, is heir to a certain classicism, he is also wedded to the realism of his figures and landscapes, whilst heralding Impressionism through his *plein-air* work.

1

2

3

Millet has been compared to the Le Nain brothers. Coming from a rural environment, it was to the humble peasants that he essentially devoted his art, having begun more as a portrait painter. Of these simple people, he creates certainly realistic figures, but also anonymous ones with their lowered faces, turning them almost into archetypes, as if he wanted to show the unchanging and sacred nature if their daily gestures. "The painting understood in this way ceases to be purely a spectacle, it is raised up and takes on a moralising, educational role; the ordinary person is channelled through the artist, and with a great, noble picture, we have a lesson in social and political morals", wrote Gambetta in 1873.

1. GUSTAVE COURBET, *Origin of the World*, 1866, oil on canvas, 46 x 55 cm
2. GUSTAVE COURBET, *Burial at Ornans*, 1849-1850, oil on canvas, 315 x 668 cm, Salon of 1850-1851
3. GUSTAVE COURBET, *The Painter's Studio. A real allegory summing up seven years of my artistic and moral existence*, 1854-1855, oil on canvas, 361 x 598 cm, "flag of realism", 1855

These works are situated on the ground floor, in Room 7.

"My aim is to create living art"

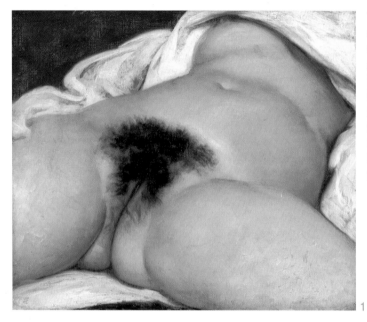

This work was bound to disturb its successive owners to such an extent that they did their utmost to reserve for themselves this both anonymous and stark piece of private life! After belonging for some time to a Turkish diplomat living in Paris who also owned *The Turkish Bath* by Ingres and who kept Courbet's nude hidden behind another landscape by the same artist, the picture disappeared from circulation. It was then acquired by a Hungarian painter who ended up selling it to the famous psychoanalyst Jacques Lacan, who also kept it hidden behind a wood panel by André Masson allusively taking up the subject of the picture.

Created by the critic Champfleury in 1847, the word "realistic" was soon used to describe the painting of Courbet who thus, almost in spite of himself, became the leader of this new school. "My aim is to be able to convey the morals, ideas and an image of my time, according to my own judgement, not only as a painter, but as a man, in a word, to create living art", wrote Courbet in 1855. He caused a real scandal with *Burial at Ornans*: all present-day subjects became not only worthy of being painted, but were entitled to the same respect as historical art. A simple burial, with very real people, merits a monumental format, as if it possessed the same universal character. No heroes here, however, just ordinary people. No idyllic view of the rural environment, either. People as they are, even if they are ugly and common.

As often, Courbet renounced the smooth appearance of academic art to show a thick, visible medium, slightly coarse brushwork which the critics hardly appreciated. On the right of the artist's central figure, his friends and supporters of Realism – Champfleury, Baudelaire, Bruyas, his friend and patron, and Proudhon.

3

1. ÉDOUARD MANET, *The Picnic*, 1863, oil on canvas, 208 x 264.5 cm, *Salon des Refusés* of 1863, under the title of *The Swim*
2. ÉDOUARD MANET, *Olympia*, 1863, oil on canvas, 130.5 x 190 cm, Salon of 1865
3. ÉDOUARD MANET, *The Fife Player*, 1866, oil on canvas, 161 x 97 cm

These works are situated on the ground floor, in Room 14, and on the top floor, in Room 29.

Manet excited criticism

Amongst the paintings shown at the Salon of the Rejected – Napoleon III had, in fact, authorised that the works which had been rejected by the official Salon should be shown in a wing at the Palais de l'Industrie on the Champs-Élysées –, was one which excited criticism: Manet's *The Swim*. As often, however, this former pupil of Thomas Couture took his inspiration from the old masters – Raphael and Titian –, but the misappropriation of a mythological episode for a common genre scene was unacceptable: this naked woman, a friend of Manet's brother, conversing in the undergrowth with two young men in ties, really had nothing in common with the classical models. As for Manet's style of painting, it was unacceptable to the majority of critics: the figures painted in flat colours, without relief or gradation, are not integrated into the landscape that is treated in an almost off-hand manner.

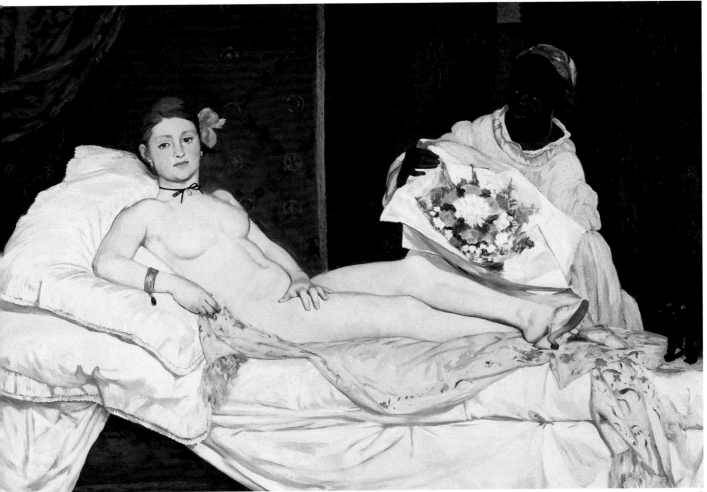

We are familiar with the copy of the *Venus of Urbino* from the Titian which Manet did in Florence in 1853 and which, with Goya's *Naked Maja*, inspired him to this *Olympia* admitted to the official Salon. But again, the citing of the old masters is misappropriated. The very real model, the same one he used for *The Swim*, Victorine Meurent, rebelliously stares out at the viewer; by placing her hand on the area she should conceal, she betrays the subject matter of the painting, confirmed by the bouquet held by the black servant, a tribute from a client. Provocative, the subject excited criticism, as did its technique, oversketched, where the black outline delimits the contours of the body handled in flat tints.

The same reproaches for this work, rejected from the Salon, in which the division into flat colours and the broad, simplified brushstrokes could not but shock most of the critics: "A second-rate drawing of a young musician, illumined by bright colours of which the red of the trousers speaks with boldness. It is applied to a monochrome grey background: no land, no sky, no perspective: the poor wretch is stuck against an imaginary wall."

3

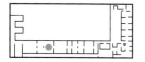

1. ÉDOUARD MANET, *Vase of Peonies on a Small Pedestal*, 1864, oil on canvas, 93.2 x 70.2 cm
2. ÉDOUARD MANET, *On the Beach*, 1873, oil on canvas, 59.6 x 73.2 cm
3. ÉDOUARD MANET, *Berthe Morisot with Bunch of Violets*, 1872, oil on canvas, 55 x 38 cm
4. ÉDOUARD MANET, *The Balcony*, 1869, oil on canvas, 170 x 124 cm

These works are situated on the ground floor, in Room 14, and on the top floor, in Room 31.

A new style of painting

Manet painted still-lifes all his life. Here, his broad, generous brushstrokes accord admirably with the sensuality and luxuriance of the peonies. When Manet was alive, the critics, who nevertheless lambasted a good number of his paintings, were often complimentary about the still-life pieces found in them, as in *Olympia* or *The Picnic*.

It is Eugène Manet, the brother of the artist and future husband of Berthe Morisot, who is shown here on the beach at Berck-sur-Mer, beside the artist's wife.

"I place nothing in Manet's work above a certain portrait of Berthe Morisot", wrote Paul Valéry, nephew by marriage of Berthe Morisot, Manet's future sister-in-law. "Through the odd harmony of the colours and the dissonance of their strengths, through the contrast of the trivial, transient detail of a hairstyle of times gone by with an indefinable sense of the tragic in the expression of the face, Manet makes his work resonate and portrays mystery in the assurance of his art. He combines the unique harmony that is appropriate for a remarkable person with the physical resemblance of the model, and strongly portrays the distinct and abstract charm of Berthe Morisot."

4

Three of Manet's friends, including Berthe Morisot, posed for *The Balcony*, it too inspired by the old masters, and in particular Goya's *Group on a Balcony*. Their diverging gazes, their treatment using flat colours, the harshness of the colours, the impression of arrested time and mystery once again shocked those looking at it. Much later, however, artists would pay tribute to this work: in a picture of the same name painted by Magritte, three coffins, including one "seated" in Berthe Morisot's place, stand behind the same guardrail, bordered by the same shutters, with the same hydrangea in its china pot.

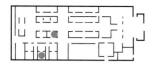

1. EUGÈNE BOUDIN, *The Beach at Trouville*, 1864, oil on wood, 26 x 48 cm
2. FRÉDÉRIC BAZILLE, *Family Gathering*, 1867, oil on canvas, 152 x 230 cm, Salon of 1868
3. PAUL GUIGOU, *The Washerwoman*, 1860, oil on canvas, 81 x 59 cm

These works are situated on the ground floor, in Rooms 14 and 20, and on the top floor, in Room 31.

The precursors of Impressionism

1

In Normandy, a number of artists, including Boudin, met at the Saint-Siméon farm where several of the painters from the Barbizon School had already worked. Originally from Honfleur, Boudin painted the Normandy coast and its landscapes: what interested this "king of the skies", according to Corot, were the atmospheric variations, and we know how much Baudelaire appreciated Boudin's numerous cloud studies. His compositions most often consist of bands of sand, sea and sky, the sky occupying the upper two thirds, whilst below, several members of fashionable society, tiny and quickly sketched, indulge in the new delights of the beach. The importance he afforded to *plein-air* painting and his palette of light colours would be of major significance in the birth of Impressionism, and specifically on Monet, who would later acknowledge his debt to Boudin and Jongkind.

2

If Boudin and his friends were more painters of atmosphere, hazy in this case, Bazille and Guigou, from the South, were, for their part, painters of light. In their works, probably influenced by certain of Courbet's canvases, the distinct shadows and spots of pure light delineate the forms and afford them stability: in that, they differ from the Impressionists, who were also interested in the light, but in order to reproduce its vibrations. Having gone to Paris, Bazille soon met, in Gleyre's studio, Renoir, Monet and Sisley, whose friend he would become and whom he supported financially. His career was all too short: he was cut down in the prime of youth during the 1870 war.

3

We find the same intensity of Mediterranean light in this work by Guigou who, like his Mediterranean compatriot, would be gone far too young, the victim of a stroke.

1. CLAUDE MONET, *The Magpie*, 1868-1869, oil on canvas, 89 x 130 cm
2. CLAUDE MONET, *Women in the Garden*, 1867, oil on canvas, 255 x 205 cm
3. CLAUDE MONET, *The Picnic*, 1865-1866, left part and right part of a composition which, left as security with a creditor, was damaged by damp and then cut out by the artist in 1884, oil on canvas, 418 x 150 cm and 248 x 217 cm

These works are situated on the ground floor, in Room 18.

Monet: colours painted hastily

This work illustrates the liking of Monet, and other Impressionists such as Pissarro, for painting the winter light and its bluish sheens on snow.

Originally from Le Havre where he met Boudin, who encoura ged him to work in the open ai Monet then went to Paris. There in Gleyre's studio, he got to know future Impressionists Renoir, Sisley and Bazille – the latter, moreover, posed here fc several figures in this composi tion. Executed in his studio during the autumn of 1865 afte he had made various sketche in the open air over the summe it heralded a new style of pain ting full-length figures sketched in spontaneous postures using broad colourful brushwork From 1867, Zacharie Astruc described Monet's pictures as being painted "hastily, in beau tiful, pure colour".

"A painting of figures, women in light-coloured summer clothes, picking flowers along a garden path; the sun fell straight onto their skirts of dazzling whiteness; the warm shadow of a tree cut across the path, on the dresses bathed in sunlight, a large grey blanket. It had the most peculiar effect." Thus commented Zola in *L'Événement illustré* of 24th May 1868, on these *Women in the Garden* by Monet in which the artist executed what, according to Zola again, is the dream of all painters: "to put full-length figures into a landscape." Unlike with *The Picnic*, Monet took an impor-tant step since he decided to sketch the composition of the picture in its final format in the open air, even though he then re-worked it in the studio.

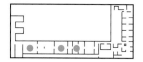

1. CLAUDE MONET, *Saint-Lazare Railway Station*, 1877, oil on canvas, 75.5 x 104 cm, 3rd Impressionist Exhibition 1877
2. CLAUDE MONET, *Rouen Cathedral. Main Door and Saint-Romain Tower, Full Sun, Harmony of Blue and Gold*, 1893, oil on canvas, 107 x 73 cm
3. CLAUDE MONET, *Study of a figure in the open air. Woman Holding an Umbrella, turning towards the left*, 1886, oil on canvas, 131 x 88 c
4. CLAUDE MONET, *Poppies*, 1873, oil on canvas, 50 x 65 cm, 1st Impressionist Exhibition, 1874

These works are situated on the top floor, in Rooms 29, 32 and 34.

"Painting the beauty of the sky"

1

2

In 1892-1893, after the *Haystacks* series, Monet began another on the theme of *Rouen Cathedral*, in which he conveyed, through rapid, coarse brush-work, the variations in the light and atmosphere on the cathedral with the passing hours and days, whilst the motif ends up almost disintegrating. Other series would follow: *London, Parliament, Views of Venice, The Waterlily Pond*…

"Our artists must discover the poetry of railway stations, just as their fathers discovered that of the forests and rivers", stated Zola. Like Turner, Daumier, Manet, Pissarro, Caillebotte and others, Monet painted these trains which had enabled them to get to the outskirts of Paris and set up their easels there in the middle of the countryside, equipped with their tubes of colours. But here, it is the inside of the station and the machines which stand out against the façades passing unnoticed behind the clouds of blue and white smoke.

Barely outlining the features of Suzanne Hoschedé, his step-daughter, Monet was keener to produce the shadow-play and the variations in the light of a fine sunny and blustery day.

3

34

4

It was at the time of the first Impressionist exhibition that the columnist of *Charivari*, Louis Leroy, hurled the neologism "impressionism" as a term of derision at the subject matter of Monet's canvas, *Impression, Sunrise*, which term was then adopted by these painters, all ridicule dispelled. Like them, another critic, Castagnary, had fully understood the extent to which this term suited these artists: "They are *impressionists* in the sense that they portray not the landscape, but the feeling produced by the landscape."

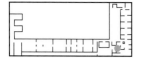

1. CLAUDE MONET, *The Artist's Garden at Giverny*, 1900, oil on canvas, 81 x 92 cm
2. CLAUDE MONET, *Lily Pond, Harmony of Pinks*, 1900, oil on canvas, 89.5 x 100 cm
3. CLAUDE MONET, *Blue Water Lilies*, 1916-1919, oil on canvas, 200 x 200 cm

These works are situated on the top floor, in Room 39.

The house at Giverny

Less than a month after setting up at Giverny in 1883, Monet wrote to Duret: "I am enraptured, Giverny is a splendid place for me to be." His infatuation for this property, which he only bought in 1890 and where he would end his days, would never cease. The many letters he sent to Alice Hoschedé – whom he married in July 1892 – when he was away travelling show this. Furthermore, he often added some snippet of advice befitting of a gardener.

1

In 1893, Monet acquired an additional plot of land on which he gradually developed his "water garden" which inspired him to a new series, *The Waterlily Pond*. "He has got himself a very small pond where the water is always clear", commented Gustave Geffroy, "he has surrounded it with trees, bushes and flowers he has chosen, and decorated its surface with different coloured waterlilies which open up in spring… Over this flower-covered water is a light wooden Japanese-style bridge, and in the water, amongst the flowers, can be seen all the sky passing by, all the air playing in the trees, all the movement of the wind, all the shades of the hours, all the stilled reflection of the surrounding natural environment."

2

3

Monet painted his garden at Giverny until he died. But over time, he became increasingly absorbed by the motif of water and waterlilies. An idea then began to germinate: that of enormous canvases "of the water, the waterlilies, the plants, but over a very big surface". These *Expansive Arrangements of Waterlilies*, which Monet donated to the State, would, in accordance with the provisions specified by the painter, be hung at the Orangerie in the Tuileries, the final legacy of an artist who, in the twilight of his life, is said to have confided to Clemenceau: "I only look at what the world has shown me, to testify to it through my brush. That's quite something, isn't it?"

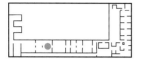

1. EDGAR DEGAS, *The Bellelli Family*, 1858-1867, oil on canvas, 200 x 250 cm, Salon of 1867
2. EDGAR DEGAS, *The Racetrack, Amateur Jockeys near a Carriage*, 1876-1887, oil on canvas, 66 x 81 cm
3. EDGAR DEGAS, *The Orchestra at the Opera*, circa 1870, oil on canvas, 56.5 x 46 cm
4. EDGAR DEGAS, *In a Café* or *Absinthe*, 1875-1876, oil on canvas, 92 x 68 cm

These works are situated on the ground floor, in Room 13, and on the top floor, in Room 31.

Degas: a classical and modern painter

Having received a classical training and copied the Italian Renaissance painters in the Louvre, Degas undertook a three-year tour in Italy. There he mixed with the great masters, but also became the friend of Gustave Moreau, who would exercise a determining influence on his development. Besides historical paintings, he did a lot of portraits at that time, most often of members of his family. In *The Bellelli Family*, a large format canvas befitting a historical painting, the artist goes beyond the simple group portrait to evoke the stifling atmosphere which prevailed at his Neopolitan cousins' home and evidenced by the letters from his aunt Laura.

Degas had gathered around the bassoonist Désiré Dihau, whom he knew well, a number of his friends – not all musicians – whom he arranged in a space where, as in Japanese prints, outlines are superimposed.

"That one will be the painter, the true painter, who will be able to draw out the epic side from life today, and make us see and understand, using colour and outline, how great and poetic we are in our ties and our polished boots." Degas soon illustrated this "heroism of modern life", as defined by Baudelaire, abandoning historical subjects. Thus it was that he painted many horse racing scenes, the fashion for this sport recently arrived from England now spreading in France. As often, he gave the impression of having taken the scene from life: in an asymmetrical composition, figures and horses enter and leave the canvas as if they had been framed for a photographic purpose – Degas used to do a lot of photography.

Degas has shown his close friend Marcellin Desboutin and the actress Hélène Andrée at the Nouvelle-Athènes café, where critics and Impressionists used to gather at that time. The resolutely modern subject and the bold technique – it looks as if the artist painted directly – shocked the critics.

4

1. EDGAR DEGAS, *Women Ironing*, 1884-1886, oil on canvas, 76 x 81.5 cm
2. EDGAR DEGAS, *Blue Dancers*, circa 1893, oil on canvas, 85 x 75.5 cm
3. EDGAR DEGAS, *The Dance Class*, 1873-1876, oil on canvas, 85 x 75 cm

These works are situated on the top floor, in Room 30 and 31.

Gestures painted from life

Degas produced several canvases on this theme which show his very acute sense of observation and his immense talent for encapsulating the life of his figures in a single gesture: "He places before our eyes, in their poses and limited charms, laundry women… speaking their language and technically explaining the *pressing* method and the *circular* method, etc.", wrote Edmond de Goncourt on 13th February 1874, the day after his visit to Degas's studio.

Another theme which insistently recurs in his work is dancing. Here, the four dancers in the foreground, painted using broad brushstrokes and vivid colours, characteristic of works at the end of his life, stand out against a mottled background which he very often used at the time. By freezing the slightly nervous gestures of each one in the act of straightening her clothes, he adds a number of extra poses to the long inventory he had created in this way throughout his career.

3

Although Degas, a very regular visitor to the Opéra, shows several dancers on stage, he usually preferred to capture a moment from a rehearsal, some ballerina straightening her tutu or readjusting her shoe or a number of dancers going up a flight of steps. His concern to produce their natural, momentary movement certainly brought him closer to the Impressionists with whom he exhibited. But all his life he rejected their primary obsession, which was to paint atmospheric changes in the open air. Degas preferred artificial light to natural light: here, uneven, it softens the forms or lends emphasis to a gesture or an accessory.

1. GUSTAVE CAILLEBOTTE, *The Planers*, 1875, oil on canvas, 102 x 146.5 cm, 2nd Impressionist Exhibition, 1876
2. HENRI FANTIN-LATOUR, *A Studio in Les Batignolles*, 1870, oil on canvas, 204 x 273.5 cm, Salon of 1870
3. JAMES TISSOT, *Portrait of Mlle L. L.* or *Young Woman in a Red Jacket*, 1864, oil on canvas, 124 x 99,5 cm, Salon of 1864
4. JAMES ABBOTT MCNEILL WHISTLER, *Arrangement in Grey and Black, No. 1* or *The Artist's Mother*, 1871, oil on canvas, 144.3 x 162.5 cm

These works are situated on the ground floor, in the Seine Gallery and in Room 15, and on the top floor, in Room 30.

Friends of the Impressionists

Even though Caillebotte, a painter of modern life, had to wait until the end of the 1870's for his technique to resemble that of his Impressionist friends, he continued to support them. It was he who, from 1876, bought the canvases of Renoir, Monet, Pissarro, Degas; it was again he who rented studios for one or another or who desperately tried to organise exhibitions. On his death, he continued to work for his friends, since he bequeathed to the State the sixty-seven Impressionist works he had collected. After three years of bitter negotiations, only thirty-eight of them were finally accepted and thus, against the uproar of some people, went into the Musée du Luxembourg, at that time the museum of living artists.

2

Although he was close to the Impressionists with whom he associated at the Café Guerbois and whom he admired, all his life Fantin-Latour kept to a traditional craft in which the outline was, more often than not, very precise. Next to his realistic still-lifes and slightly magical compositions, he excelled in the art of the portrait, whether individual or group. Around Manet, seated and in the process of painting, are gathered painters and critics, all ardent defenders of modernity – Renoir, Bazille, Monet, but also Astruc and Zola.

Over some fifteen years, Tissot was the friend of Degas, who painted his portrait. However, Tissot's liking for a meticulous finish and a porcelained medium was decidedly nothing like Degas's style.

4

A close friend of Fantin-Latour, the American painter Whistler also associated with Courbet and Manet when he came to France from London, where he was based. But his art, which remained realistic, was more influenced by Japanese art: as in the prints which he collected, he simplified the lines, flattened the space and often cut down his palette.

3

1. PIERRE-AUGUSTE RENOIR, *Study. Torso: Effects of Sunlight*, 1875-1876, oil on canvas, 81 x 65 cm, 2nd Impressionist Exhibition, 187
2. PIERRE-AUGUSTE RENOIR, *Dancing at the Moulin de la Galette, Montmartre*, 1876, oil on canvas, 131 x 175 cm, 3rd Impressionist Exhibition, 1877
3. PIERRE-AUGUSTE RENOIR, *The Swing*, 1876, oil on canvas, 92 x 73 cm, 3rd Impressionist Exhibition, 1877

These works are situated on the top floor, in Room 32.

Renoir: bursts of sunlight

Trained in Gleyre's studio, where he made the acquaintance of Monet and Bazille, Renoir, like his Impressionist friends, was interested in the variations of light. But, unlike Monet, it was above all the human form that he enjoyed painting, with a marked preference for the female nude: "I am a painter of the figure", he maintained. This bust demonstrates the fact and, with a few rare exceptions, enraged the critics: "Please try, therefore, to explain to M. Renoir that the female torso is not a mass of decomposing flesh with green and purple blotches denoting a state of complete putrefaction in a cadaver", wrote Albert Wolff in *Le Figaro*. The very bold brushwork, which depicts a background of almost abstract foliage and makes the light flicker on the torso of the nude woman, could not fail to exasperate most of his contemporaries for whom the finished appearance of the picture was vital. At this time, Renoir was no longer drawing: he painted splashes of juxtaposed colours.

1

Several sketches preceded this major composition which Renoir probably executed on the spot, in Montmartre. Unlike the work he was doing until then, he includes a large number of figures, to portray lots of friends, in which the contours, once again, seem to disappear in a vivid vibration of colour. A common thread between these three canvases is that they were purchased by the friend of the Impressionists, also a painter himself, Gustave Caillebotte.

44

2

3

The Swing was the subject of criticism of the same kind: Renoir's brush seems
to break up forms, and the patches of light filtering through the foliage to accen-
tuate the painting could only shock the public, even though some of Renoir's
friends found the canvas charming.

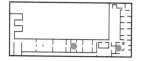

1. PIERRE-AUGUSTE RENOIR, *Dancing in the Countryside*, 1883, oil on canvas, 180 x 90 cm
2. PIERRE-AUGUSTE RENOIR, *Dancing in the Town*, 1883, oil on canvas, 180 x 90 cm
3. PIERRE-AUGUSTE RENOIR, *Young Girls at the Piano*, 1892, oil on canvas, 116 x 90 cm
4. PIERRE-AUGUSTE RENOIR, *Women Bathing*, 1918-1919, oil on canvas, 110 x 160 cm

These works are situated on the top floor, in Rooms 34 and 39.

Between drawing and colour

1

2

The elegant model who posed for *Dancing in the Town* was a young girl of seventeen, Marie-Clémentine Valadon, who would soon become famous as a painter by the name of Suzanne Valadon, mother of another painter, Maurice Utrillo.

From the 1880's, Renoir, like several other Impressionists, wondered about the effect of dissolving forms which led to the practice of fragmented brushwork. "I had got to the end of Impressionism and I realised that I could neither paint nor draw", he was to tell Vollard later. The trip he made to Italy in 1881 and reflection on the works of Raphael and the remains of Pompeii also showed him "that grandeur and simplicity of the early painters". Thus it was that, on his return, he produced several canvases in which the principal forms were clearly defined. In these two dance scenes, designed to create a pair, both couples are distinctly drawn, even though, in some parts of the picture – the background foliage or the dress in *Dancing in the Town* –, colour very freely continues to shape the forms.

This theme, which he approached for the first time around 1875 was one of Renoir's favourite subjects. An impression of harmony and serenity emanates from this work acquired by the State the same year it was executed.

3

Another recurrent theme with Renoir was women bathing. In shaping these more recent bathers in warm colours using soft and rounded brushstrokes which blend them into the very boldly painted landscape, Renoir seems to have totally abandoned the slightly hard lines and the dry brushwork which depicted his earlier bathers of the years around 1885. Considered his pictorial legacy, they are a restatement, near the end of his life, of the delight and joie de vivre so often present in his work.

4

1. ALFRED SISLEY, *The Regatta at Molesey*, 1874, oil on canvas, 66 x 91.5 cm
2. CAMILLE PISSARRO, *Red Roofs, Corner of the Village, Effects of Winter*, 1877, oil on canvas, 54.5 x 65.6 cm, 3rd Impressionist Exhibition, 1877
3. BERTHE MORISOT, *The Cradle*, 1872, oil on canvas, 56 x 46 cm, 1st Impressionist Exhibition, 1874
4. MARY CASSATT, *Woman Sewing a Garden*, 1880-1882, oil on canvas, 92 x 63 cm, 8th Impressionist Exhibition, 1886

These works are situated on the top floor, in Rooms 30 and 32.

Outside and in

Throughout his life, Sisley, born in Paris of English parents and a great admirer of Constable and Turner, painted almost only landscapes. Originally influenced by Daubigny and Corot, he gradually adopted the Impressionist style. In this canvas, the tiny silhouettes are put in using tiny brushstrokes, whilst broad grey outlines sweep the sky, heralding imminent rain from across the Channel. The wind lifting up the flags finishes giving the scene its snapshot character.

1

Originally influenced by Daubigny, Corot and even Courbet, Pissarro was soon pursuing the same sort of research as his Impressionist friends in his Île-de-France landscapes. His art is different, however: the composition of his canvases is more confident, and he is less interested in showing changes in sky or water than concerned with the land and, often, those working on it. Like others, he would go through a crisis at the start of the 1880's and, around 1885, adopt the pointillist technique developed by Seurat, before returning to his earlier style.

2

48

A friend of Corot, Berthe Morisot soon met Manet – whose brother she married in 1874 –, but also Monet, Bazille and Renoir. Like them, she painted in the open air, but all her life she retained a marked preference for portraits and scenes of tender intimacy in which she would often show her close relations – here, her sister and niece.

3

After a grand tour of Europe where she copied the old masters, the American Mary Cassatt spent most of her career in France where, having become the friend of Degas, she joined the Impressionists. Like Berthe Morisot, but even more exclusively and in meticulous, static compositions, she painted middle-class women and children in a still, peaceful environment. She would also, inevitably, contribute to the spread of Impressionism in her country of origin.

4

1. PAUL CÉZANNE, *Self-Portrait*, 1873-1876, oil on canvas, 64 x 53 cm
2. PAUL CÉZANNE, *House of the Hanged Man*, 1873, oil on canvas, 55 x 66 cm, 1st Impressionist Exhibition, 1874
3. PAUL CÉZANNE, *L'Estaque*, 1878-1879, oil on canvas, 59.5 x 73 cm

These works are situated on the top floor, in Room 36.

Cézanne's early work

This self-portrait, painted using long, thick strokes, reveals Cézanne as slightly coarse and grouchy.

1

After early paintings depicting violent themes and painted in a savage style with a heavily-loaded brush, Cézanne, from the South of France, met Pissarro who, around 1872, invited him to come and work alongside him at Pontoise then at Auvers-sur-Oise, and who initiated him into the Impressionist principles: working outdoors, and light, broken brushwork. *House of the Hanged Man* clearly illustrates how, even in this period described as "Impressionist", the art of Cézanne remains different from that of Monet and Renoir: rather than capture the ephemeral and the fleeting through an effervescent style, Cézanne endeavours to produce, by dense, grainy brushwork, the structure of objects, the depth of volumes and the balance of the composition using geometric shapes.

2

3

A few months before his death, Cézanne stated to Maurice Denis that he had "wanted to make Impressionism solid and durable, like the art of the museums". Even though this landscape of *L'Estaque* was painted on the motif, Cézanne distanced himself in relation to what he was looking at so as to construct a timeless and in some way classical scene: in a composition based on parallel, perpendicular and oblique lines, small parallel and regular brushstrokes add volume to the houses, roofs, trees and mountains, whilst the blue sea is handled using flat colour. "There are two things in the painter," he said, "the eye and the brain. They must help one another. The artist must work on developing both: the eye by looking at nature, and the brain through the logic of organised sensations, which produces the means of expression."

1. PAUL CÉZANNE, *The Card Players*, 1890-1895, oil on canvas, 47.5 x 57 cm
2. PAUL CÉZANNE, *Bathers*, 1890-1892, oil on canvas, 60 x 82 cm
3. PAUL CÉZANNE, *Woman with Coffee-Pot*, 1890-1895, oil on canvas, 130.5 x 96.5 cm
4. PAUL CÉZANNE, *Apples and Oranges*, 1895-1900, oil on canvas, 74 x 93 cm

These works are situated on the top floor, in Room 36 and in the Heights Gallery.

Cylinder, sphere and cone

Taking up a theme from 17th century art, Cézanne positions the two men, motionless and serious, farm labourers from Jas de Bouffan, Cézanne's family estate, around a bottle which serves as the axis of symmetry for this composition.

During the last fifteen years of his life, Cézanne relentlessly took up the same motifs – Mont Sainte-Victoire, male or female bathers.

In his many portraits, inflicting long posing sessions on his models, Cézanne waited for what he called his "minute sensation", which he experienced after endless hours of observation and which enabled him to construct his picture. "Painting nature is to create its sensations", he used to say. To his wife, of whom he painted more than twenty portraits and who sometimes became somewhat impatient, he replied: "Do the apples move?" In *Woman with Coffee-Pot*, Cézanne reconstructed the portrait of the woman through simple geometric shapes. It was necessary to "handle nature using the cylinder, the sphere and the cone": a cylinder for the cup and coffee-pot, a pyramid cone for the woman, "sitting firm like an imposing tower", slightly tilted rectangles for the door-panels.

4

"I want to amaze Paris with an apple", Cézanne had said. In his still-lifes, he portrayed the fruit and objects he had chosen. Here, arranged around an ascending diagonal line which travels across the entire painting, the objects, perceived from different viewpoints, appear to tilt forward according to a fanciful perspective. "Art is harmony in parallel with nature", he used to day: in other words, the painter's task is not to give the illusion of reality, but to reconstruct another convincing reality from it, where the picture is only a flat, vertical surface. Cézanne thus paved the way for the major innovative movements of the early 20th century, Fauvism and Cubism.

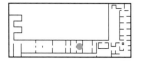

1. VINCENT VAN GOGH, *The Italian Woman*, 1887, oil on canvas, 81 x 60 cm
2. VINCENT VAN GOGH, *The Woman from Arles*, 1888, oil on canvas, 92.5 x 73.5 cm
3. VINCENT VAN GOGH, *The Dance Hall at Arles*, 1888, oil on canvas, 65 x 81 cm
4. VINCENT VAN GOGH, *Starry Night*, 1888, oil on canvas, 72.5 x 92 cm

These works are situated on the top floor, in Room 35.

Van Gogh in the light of the South

1

It was only at the age of twenty-seven that Van Gogh chose to become a painter. Arriving in Paris at the end of February 1886, he encountered for the first time a style of painting that was completely different to his own, both in terms of subjects and palette. "In Anvers, I never even knew what the Impressionist paintings were; now I've seen them." He very quickly absorbed what the Impressionists had to teach, but also learned from Gauguin, Seurat and Signac. In this portrait of Agostina Segatori, the model, who stands out, devoid of depth, against the yellow background, is painted in outlines of strong, random colours: the painter has achieved the objective he had set himself at that time, "to apply increasingly vivid colours".

"I've finally got a woman from Arles", wrote Van Gogh after finishing this portrait of Marie Ginoux, whose husband kept the café where Van Gogh ate every day.

When he had left Paris a few months earlier, Van Gogh had hoped that other artists would come and join him in Arles where they would have started a joint studio. But Gauguin was the only one to come, and his stay ended dramatically: on 23rd December, a violent argument broke out between the two men, at the end of which Van Gogh cut off his ear. Gauguin's influence is perceptible in this picture – simplified forms, dark outlines defining the contours and the use of flat colours.

3

4

"I went for a walk one night," he wrote to his brother, Theo. "The deep blue sky was dotted with clouds of a blue deeper than the primal blue of intense cobalt, and others of a lighter blue, like the blue-white of the Milky Way. The stars flickered against the blue background, clear, greeny, yellow, white, lighter pinks, more set with diamonds like precious stones than we are – even in Paris…: opals, emeralds, lapises, rubies, sapphires."

1. VINCENT VAN GOGH, *Van Gogh's Bedroom at Arles*, 1889, oil on canvas, 57.5 x 74 cm
2. VINCENT VAN GOGH, *Meridian* or *Siesta, after Millet*, 1889-1890, oil on canvas, 73 x 91 cm
3. VINCENT VAN GOGH, *Hôpital Saint-Paul in Saint-Rémy-de-Provence*, 1889, oil on canvas, 63 x 48 cm
4. VINCENT VAN GOGH, *Portrait of the Artist*, 1889, oil on canvas, 65 x 54.5 cm

These works are situated on the top floor, in Rooms 35 and 50.

From Arles to Saint-Rémy-de-Provence

Van Gogh painted this third version of the bedroom he occupied at Arles whilst he was in Saint-Rémy-de-Provence: after a violent fit in which he threatened Gauguin, he asked to be committed to an asylum very near Saint-Rémy. There, he worked again without respite. In his paintings, the colour, besides its descriptive character, suggests various sentiments. He wrote to Theo about *The Bedroom*: "In a word, looking at the picture ought to rest the brain, or rather the imagination… The broad lines of the furniture, again, must express absolute rest."

In the only study on Van Gogh's painting that appeared during his lifetime, Albert Aurier alluded to "the trees twisted like giants in battle… What characterises his entire work is excess, excess force, excess nervous tension, the violence of the expression."

"For me, it is not Manet who is the exceedingly modern painter, but Millet who, for a lot of people, worked distant perspectives", wrote Van Gogh who, all his life, admired and copied the works of his predecessor.

4

"I didn't have the money to pay models, otherwise I would have devoted myself entirely to painting figures", wrote Van Gogh in 1886. Is this the reason why, like his fellow country-man Rembrandt, he so often took himself as the model, depicting himself with hard, bony features, his gaze always inquisitorial?

1. VINCENT VAN GOGH, *Thatches at Cordeville, at Auvers-sur-Oise*, 1890, oil on canvas, 73 x 92 cm
2. VINCENT VAN GOGH, *Dr. Paul Gachet*, 1890, oil on canvas, 68 x 57 cm
3. VINCENT VAN GOGH, *The Church at Auvers-sur-Oise*, view of apse, 1890, oil on canvas, 94 x 74.5 cm

These works are situated on the top floor, in Room 35.

The last months at Auvers

1

When he arrived in Auvers-sur-Oise on 20th May 1890, Van Gogh was captivated by this little village, and he painted a great number of landscapes at that time: his energetic brushwork made it one of the most successful.

2

In Auvers, Van Gogh painted several portraits of Dr. Gachet, about which he wrote: "I *would like…* to paint portraits which, a century later, seem like apparitions to the people living then. So I do not attempt to paint a photographic representation, but rather our passionate expressions, using, as a vehicle for expression and exaltation of the character, our modern science and taste for colour. Hence, in the portrait of Dr. Gachet you see a face the colour of a red-hot, sun-burnt brick, with red hair, a white hat framed by a landscape of blue hills in the background, his clothes are ultra-marine blue - they make his face stand out and turn it pale despite its brick-red colour. His hands, the hands of a man who delivers babies, are paler than his face."

3

"With that I have a bigger painting of the village church – an effect where the building looks purplish against a sky of ultramarine blue, the roof is violet and partly orange-coloured. In the foreground, a touch of flowering greenery and pink sun-soaked sand. It's again the same as in the studies I made in Nuenen of the old tower and the cemetery, only now the colour is probably more expressive, more sumptuous." Although the pink of the path has now disappeared, the strength and vigour of the colours and forms remain intact. A few weeks later, on 29th July, at the age of thirty-seven, Van Gogh committed suicide: his career had lasted only ten years.

1. ÉMILE BERNARD, *Madeleine in the Bois d'Amour*, 1888, oil on canvas, 138 x 163 cm
2. PAUL SÉRUSIER, *The Talisman*, 1888, oil on canvas, 27 x 21.5 cm; inscription on the reverse: "Painted in October 1888 under the direction of Gauguin by P. Sérusier, Pont-Aven"
3. PAUL GAUGUIN, *Self-Portrait with Yellow Christ*, 1889-1890, oil on canvas, 38 x 46 cm
4. PAUL GAUGUIN, *The Beautiful Angèle*, 1889, oil on canvas, 92 x 73 cm

These works are situated on the top floor, in Rooms 43 and 48.

A revolution in Pont-Aven

After beginning with Impressionist works, Gauguin sought to find his way. During the summer of 1888, his encounter in Pont-Aven with Émile Bernard, whose style of painting was quite unlike that of the Impressionists, would at that time be a determining factor. For him, artists should paint not the motif, but from their memories. Thus freed from the primacy of observing nature, distorted lines, partitioned forms and random flat colours should yield only to the symbolic significance of the painting. Fascinated, Gauguin assimilated all Bernard's principles. It is he who, wrongly, would be considered the inventor of Symbolism.

1

In the autumn of 1888, Paul Sérusier was also in Pont-Aven. It was there that, under "dictation" from Gauguin, he painted a small landscape, an event recounted several years later by Maurice Denis: "How do you see that tree?", Gauguin had asked at a corner of the Bois d'Amour. "Green? Then paint it green, the most beautiful green on your palette. And that shadow? I would say blue. Don't be afraid of painting it as blue as possible." That painting lesson which advocated liberating colour and unfettering the painter from the motif would soon be decisive for the Nabis when, on returning from Pont-Aven, Sérusier showed them the little painting.

2

3

In this quite faithful self-portrait, painted a few months before he first left for Tahiti, Gauguin depicts himself firstly as an artist in front of two of his works, *The Yellow Christ* and *The Tobacco Jar*. The parallel hatching owes much to Cézanne.

"How awful!" declared Angèle Satre to Gauguin when she finally saw the informal portrait the painter had done: Angèle's parents ran a café near the Gloanec guesthouse, where Gauguin was staying that summer. Rejected by its model – a good portrait is necessarily first and foremost a close likeness –, it was Degas who bought it in 1891 and kept it until his death.

4

1. PAUL GAUGUIN, *The Meal* or *The Bananas*, 1891, oil on paper re-mounted on canvas, 73 x 92 cm
2. PAUL GAUGUIN, *Tahitian Women* or *On the Beach*, 1891, oil on canvas, 69 x 91.5 cm
3. PAUL GAUGUIN, *The White Horse*, 1898, oil on canvas, 140 x 91.5 cm

These works are situated on the top floor, in Room 44.

Gauguin: the renewal of the islands

This scene is the pretext for a magnificent still-life arranged in the foreground, where dishes, fruit and utensils seem to have been chosen first and foremost for their decorative qualities.

2

"Don't trust the model", advised Gauguin to his followers. "The simple stained-glass window attracting the eye by its divisions of colours and forms is the best thing. Don't copy from nature. Art is an abstraction." In fact, the lines and the colours of his paintings were from now on quite unconnected with what he was observing. In *Tahitian Women*, nothing guarantees that these two women are sitting on the beach, contrary to the suggestion of the other title given to the canvas: the strips of colour in the background cannot be interpreted with certainty. As for the lines of the bodies, Gauguin did not hesitate to distort them to express the silent, melancholic heaviness of these motionless women: "Always this silence. I understand why these people can remain hours, days, sitting without saying a word, looking melancholically at the sky."

After a rather disappointing return to France – the sale he had organised there was a failure –, Gauguin departed again a final time to Tahiti, then to the Marquesas Islands, from which he would not return. It was again in Tahiti that he painted *The White Horse*, the first of a series he devoted at that period to this animal. The naked, unfettered riders painted in lavish colours give this idyllic landscape an appearance of paradise, whereas Gauguin was going through a period of great despair.

3

1. Pierre Puvis de Chavannes, *Summer*, 1873, oil on canvas, 350 x 507 cm
2. Pierre Puvis de Chavannes, *The Poor Fisherman*, 1881, oil on canvas, 155.5 x 192.5 cm
3. Paul Gauguin, *Their Glowing Golden Bodies*, 1901, oil canvas, 67 x 76 cm
4. Pierre Puvis de Chavannes, *Young Girls by the Sea*, 1879, oil on canvas, 205 x 154 cm

These works are situated on the ground floor, in Room 11, and on the top floor, in Room 44.

Pierre Puvis de Chavannes

Following a trip to Italy in 1847 which decided his vocation, Puvis de Chavannes briefly visited the studio of Delacroix and Couture. But it was perhaps another painter who influenced him most, Chassériau, with the frescoes, which are gone today, that he had made for the staircase of the Audit Office. Following in his footsteps, Puvis, from the 1860's onwards, created massive decorative works – canvases painted in the studio and then mounted – commissioned by the State for a great many public monuments in Paris and the provinces.

"Puvis overwhelms me with his talent", wrote Gauguin, who was still saying that he dreamed of doing a "colourful Puvis" in Tahiti and who, in one of his still-lifes, had painted a copy of *Hope*. It is easy to understand the affinities which might link Gauguin to a painter who said of himself: "I wanted to become more temperate and simpler and simpler. I condensed, epitomised, compressed. I endeavoured to make each gesture express something. I tried to say as much in as few words as possible."

Puvis also painted easel canvases, often fairly faithful replicas of certain elements of his big mural paintings, sometimes depicting independent subjects, like this *Poor Fisherman*, which shows the characteristic features of his style: primacy of the line, lack of relief, simplification of forms, balanced composition, matt and light colours that express timeless feelings rather than depict a realistic, anecdotal situation. "A work," Puvis used to say, "is born out of a sort of confused emotion in which it is contained, like an animal from an egg. I take the thought which lies in an emotion, and I roll it and roll it, until it becomes clear before my eyes and I see it as sharply as possible. Then I look for a view which precisely reflects this... This is Symbolism, if you like."

64

4

An official artist if ever there was one and whose work nowadays seems under-estimated, Puvis was
for a long time, however, rejected by the Salon, regularly slated by the critics and fiercely defended by
the most innovative painters – the Symbolists, naturally, such as Redon, Hammershoï or Hodler, but also
Seurat, Signac, Cross, Van Gogh, Gauguin, the Nabis, Maillol, Munch, Matisse and even... Picasso.

1. HENRI DE TOULOUSE-LAUTREC, *Jane Avril Dancing*, 1891, oil or paint mixed with spirits on cardboard, 85.5 x 45 cm
2. HENRI DE TOULOUSE-LAUTREC, *Louis Bouglé*, 1898, oil on wood, 63 x 51 cm
3. HENRI DE TOULOUSE-LAUTREC, *Dancing at the Moulin-Rouge (La Goulue and Valentin le Désossé)*, panel for La Goulue's booth, at the Foire du Trône in Paris, 1895, oil on canvas, 298 x 316 cm
4. HENRI DE TOULOUSE-LAUTREC, *Woman at Her Toilet* or *Redhead*, 1896, oil on cardboard, 67 x 54 cm

These works are situated on the top floor, in the Heights Gallery and in Room 47.

The world of Toulouse-Lautrec

To those who reproched the excessiv speed with whic he executed his po traits – a few se sions were enoug for him –, the grea portrait painter tha he was retorte that "the expression [must] prevail ov the figure".

1

2

Less ostentatious and more elegant than La Goulue, Jane Avril, "the embodiment of dance", according to Arsène Houssaye, was nicknamed Melinite, after a powerful explosive. "Jane Avril was dancing, turning, graceful and light, a little eccentric, pale and slender, a thoroughbred," related Paul Leclercq. "Lautrec was loudly voicing his admiration." The painter has focused on the figure in the foreground all the brilliance of his rapid, spirited and remarkably assured brush, leaving bare some areas of the brown canvas which makes up the background.

The world in which the aristocrat Toulouse Lautrec lived and which he painted cou not be further from his original back ground. It was from the most divers dance halls of Montmartre, the live-mus cafés, circuses, cabarets, theatres an brothels that he in fact drew his inspira tion. In 1895, having decided to appea at the Foire du Trône in a belly-dance rou tine, La Goulue asked the artist to pai two panels to decorate the entrance to h booth. *Dancing at the Moulin-Roug* evokes that past era when, with her par ner, Valentin le Désossé, she used dance the very popular *chahut*, unbridle leg movements of which were conside red obscene by some people.

3

4

Whilst the exact subject of this work has not been identified with certainty, the theme of the woman at her toilet, the perspective viewed from above and the framing where the woman is seen from the back going about her daily life connect Toulouse-Lautrec with Degas, for whom he vouched great admiration.

1. ODILON REDON, *Closed Eyes*, 1890, oil on canvas on wood, 44 x 36 cm
2. EUGÈNE CARRIÈRE, *The Sick Child*, 1885, oil on canvas, 200 x 246 cm
3. HENRI ROUSSEAU, know as LE DOUANIER ROUSSEAU, *The Snake Charmer*, 1907, oil on canvas, 169 x 189.5 cm

These works are situated on the middle floor, in Room 59, and on the top floor, in Rooms 40 and 42.

Apart
from the movements of their times

From his first albums of lithographs and his charcoal drawings, his "Blacks", as he called them, Redon stirred the admiration of a great many Symbolist writers: Huysmans, but also Mallarmé, Gide and Valéry. Although he never gave up drawing, from 1890, he "espoused" colour, as he himself said, in paintings, pastels and watercolours, never leaving "the ambiguous world of the indeterminate" where mystery and the bizarre lead towards the banks of the unconscious.

1

Somewhat overlooked nowadays, whereas he was much admired by the public and critics of his time, this former lithographer's apprentice, influenced by the pastels of La Tour and by Turner, drew his inspiration above all from his family. His scenes of private life and anxious tenderness, on the edge of sentimentalism, painted in ochre, grey and brown tones, are bathed in a bistre haze. Carrière also painted portraits of Verlaine, Alphonse Daudet, Gustave Geffroy and Edmond de Goncourt.

2

3

Fifteen years before his death, probably concerned with the image he would leave to posterity, Rousseau drafted an autobiographical note: "But it is in the end an exotic world with lush vegetation, invented from nothing, inhabited by completely unthreatening wild animals, that has been left by this painter, friend to Apollinarius, who was perhaps more naïve in his life than in his art, and who could appeal to several of the great artists of the 20th century: Delaunay, Kandinsky, Picasso." Perhaps it was the painter himself who was the most qualified to define his painting in the artistic world of those days.

These works are situated on the middle floor, in Rooms 60 and 62.

Fin de siècle abroad

1

After training at the Académie de Bruxelles which hardly suited him, Ensor, Belgian by birth, influenced in his early work by Impressionnism, painted a whole series of intimist subjects during the 1880's, such as *Lady in Distress*, originally entitled *Troubled*. Neither of these titles really explains the painting: even though the environment is comfortable and hushed, the lack of a subject lends the canvas a mysterious atmosphere which the treatment of the light renders almost disturbing. As often, he took as a model one of his close relations, here, his sister Mitche. Ensor would soon abandon this intimist vein to portray grotesque figures, carnival masques and sneering skeletons in the Flemish tradition of a Hieronymus Bosch.

2

In 1848, a number of young artists, describing themselves as "Pre-Raphaelite Brothers", came together: fired by the desire to rediscover spontaneous art, symbolised as they saw it by the painters who preceded Raphael, they wanted to return to the simplicity of the Italian Primitives, untrained in the classical rules of the Renaissance. Some ten years later, Burne-Jones associated himself with this movement, although, in *The Wheel of Fortune*, the pose and anatomy of the figures are directly linked to the art of Michelangelo, whom he had probably admired during his many trips to Italy.

Often considered one of the precursors of Expressionism, the Norwegian painter Edvard Munch heralds here, through the strong contrast in the colours making up this landscape, the Fauvist canvases which would upset the critics at the Salon d'Automne in Paris a year later.

3

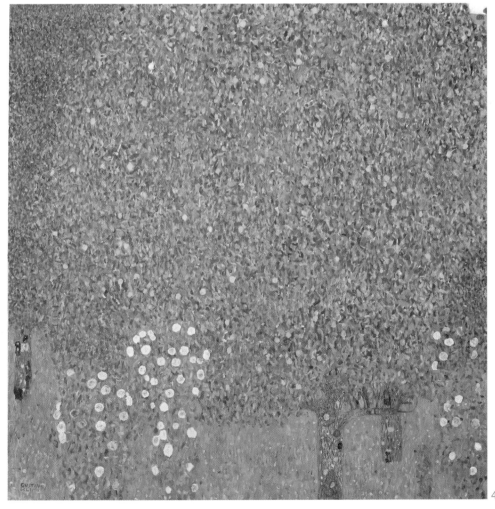

The first Chairman and one of the founders of Sezession, the Viennese version of Art Nouveau, Klimt is especially known for his oil paintings and for his large decorative paintings executed for many buildings – museums, exhibition centres, private residences and theatres –, the eroticism of which often sparked off a scandal. From 1900 onwards, however, he produced numerous landscapes devoid of any perspective to which pointillist touches of vivid colour lent an ornamental mosaic appearance.

4

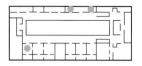

1. PIERRE BONNARD, *Woman with Checked Dress*, 1891, tempera on paper re-mounted on canvas, 160 x 48 cm
2. PIERRE BONNARD, *Child Playing in the Sand*, circa 1894, tempera mixed with glue on canvas, 167 x 50 cm
3. PIERRE BONNARD, *The Dressing-Table* or *The Mirror*, 1908, oil on canvas, 52.5 x 45.5 cm
4. MAURICE DENIS, *The Muses*, 1893, oil on canvas, 171.5 x 137.5 cm

These works are situated on the middle floor, in Rooms 65, 70 and 72.

Bonnard and Maurice Denis

Japonism, too, for this other piece of a screen on which Bonnard painted a family scene: on holiday, he was in the habit of sketching and photographing his nephews and nieces at play.

2

"There are no more paintings, only decorations. We need walls to draw on", declared the Nabis. Producing prints, posters, stage settings, decorative panels and furniture or stained-glass designs, Bonnard illustrates this desire to integrate art with life. The clearly visible contour which outlines this silhouette, the lack of depth and relief, the random space, sinuous lines, expressive distortions, geometric motifs such as the draughtboard and the format in terms of height and even what it was originally designed for – the folding screen – owe much to Japanese art: in 1892, the critic Félix Fénéon nick-named Bonnard the "Japanese Nabi".

1

As in *The Dressing-Room Mirror*, from the Pushkin Museum in Moscow, Bonnard used a mirror to expand the space and show what the person looking at the painting ought not to see: a naked woman getting washed, a theme which he would continue to take up and of which the "Nudes in the Bath", a few years later, form possibly his most accomplished works.

3

Whilst Sérusier may be considered the founder of the Nabi movement, Maurice Denis, the "Nabi of the beautiful icons", in drafting a manifesto of the Nabi style at the age of twenty, became its theoretician. It was in this that he gave a completely new and innovative definition of painting: "It must be remembered that a painting, before becoming a war-horse, a naked woman or any other anecdote, is essentially a flat surface covered with colours assembled in a certain order."

4

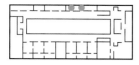

1. ÉDOUARD VUILLARD, *The Nannies, The Conversation, Red Umbrella*, 1894, paint mixed with glue on canvas, 213.5 x 73 + 154 + 81
panel depicting the *Public Gardens* commissioned to decorate the dining-room of Alexandre Natanson's private residence in Paris
2. ÉDOUARD VUILLARD, *In Bed*, 1891, oil on canvas, 73 x 92.5 cm
3. FÉLIX VALLOTTON, *The Ball*, 1899, oil on cardboard glued onto wood, 48 x 61 cm

These works are situated on the middle floor, in Rooms 70 and 71.

Vuillard and Valloton

Vuillard shared with the Nabis the plan of "putting art into life". Thus it was that he designed sets and programmes for their friend Lugné-Poe's Théâtre de l'Œuvre, illustrated several literary works and accepted various commissions for decorative paintings: he produced nine panels for Alexandre Natanson, – five of which are in the Orsay –, on which he used a new technique, sizing or paint mixed with glue, which enabled him to obtain a matt effect and which he would then use in his easel paintings. Like Bonnard, with whom he shared time in a studio, he was influenced by Japanese prints: arabesques, undulating contours outlining forms, lack of perspective and relief.

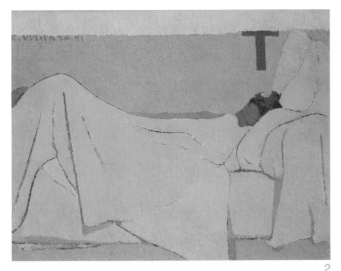

The broad flat pastel colours which break up the forms geometrically illustrate to perfection the principles observed by the Nabis. In 1895, Denis wrote about them: "In their work, they favoured expression through décor, through the harmony of forms and colours, and the medium used, rather than expression through the subject. They believed that for every emotion, for every human thought, a decorative, plastic equivalent exists, with matching beauty."

2

3

On arriving in Paris, the Swiss-born Vallotton entered the Académie Julian, where he met the Nabis. He soon became the illustrator for many magazines, including *La Revue blanche* published by the Natanson brothers. His works, whose simplification probably stems from his knowledge of engraving, are often imprinted with a certain anxiousness: here, the imposing mass of foliage and shadows, compared with the two tiny silhouettes of the women and the lone child in a perspective seen from above, create a mysterious, overwhelming impression.

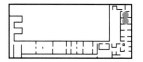

1. GEORGES SEURAT, *The Circus*, 1891, oil on canvas, 185.5 x 152.5 cm
2. PAUL SIGNAC, *Red Buoy*, 1895, oil on canvas, 81 x 65 cm
3. HENRI-EDMOND DELACROIX, known as HENRI-EDMOND CROSS, *Evening Air*, 1893-1894, oil on canvas, 116 x 165 cm
4. HENRI MATISSE, *Luxury, Quietness, and Pleasure*, 1904, oil on canvas, 98.5 x 118.5 cm

These works are situated on the top floor, in Rooms 45 and 46.

Scientific Impressionism

1

In inventing "Divisionism", in other words, in painting with tiny, evenly juxtaposed dots of pure colour, Seurat was trying, in his way, to provide a solution for the disappearing forms with which Impressionism had ended up. In *The Circus*, painted in a divided-up style, the lines of the skilfully arranged composition express sentiments – the horizontal lines evoke immobility, the ascending oblique lines, dynamism… Seurat died before seeing his painting hung at the Salon des Indépendants: he was thirty-two, and it was Signac who would take up the torch of this new pictorial technique, dubbed Neo-Impressionism.

After early works much influenced by the Impressionism of Monet and Pissarro, Signac adopted Seurat's Divisionism, even though, in this seascape, he is fairly free in relation to the "small dots": the brushwork is less systematic, slightly more straightforward and spontaneous. Passionately fond of boating, he painted the sea and ports – here, Saint-Tropez – all through his life.

2

Many painters quickly went to join Seurat: Dubois-Pillet, Angrand, Luce, Cross, who had also settled in the South and often painted alongside Signac, and even old Pissarro. A few Belgian painters joined this small group, such as Lemmen and Van Rysselberghe. Over time, these artists would distance themselves in relation to this new technique invented by "juvenile little chemists who accumulate little dots", terms in which Gaugin had described in Seurat and Signac.

3

It was at Saint-Tropez, during the summer of 1904, that Matisse, having met Signac, learned from him how to use pure colour with juxtaposed brushstrokes, a technique he would soon abandon: from the following year, he would devote himself to the explosion of Fauvist colours.

4

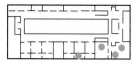

1. WILLIAM BOUGUEREAU, *The Birth of Venus*, 1879, oil on canvas, 300 x 215 cm, Salon of 1879
2. HENRI GERVEX, *Session of the Painting Jury*, 1885, oil on canvas, 299 x 419 cm, *Salon des Artistes Français*, 1885
3. GIOVANNI BOLDINI, *Count Robert de Montesquiou*, 1897, oil on canvas, 160 x 82.5 cm
4. LÉON BONNAT, *Mme Pasca*, 1874, oil on canvas, 222.5 x 132 cm

These works are situated on the middle floor, in Rooms 51, 52, 53 and 57.

The official art of the Third Republic

Whilst the role of tradespeople increasingly grew from the 1870's, the Salon system was still so rooted in what was held to be the usual practice that most painters tried to get their canvases exhibited there, even when their chances were small: "There are, in Paris, scarcely fifteen art lovers capable of appreciating a painter without the Salon", wrote Renoir to Durand-Ruel in 1881. In this "Jury Session" painted by Gervex, some of the jurors can be recognised: Bouguereau, Puvis de Chavannes, Guillaumet, Carolus-Duran, Cormon… even Gervex himself, all well in with the officials.

1

In the tradition of Ingres and Cabanel, Bouguereau continued to select his subjects from Antiquity and triumphed in the Salon of 1879 with this languid, affected and falsely modest Venus, softly lifting her locks. The smooth, glazed brushstrokes, admired by the supporters of official art, would be scoffed at by others: "A badly bloated windbag…, she's got no muscles or nerves or blood…; it's a miracle of balance that the poor wretch stays upright. One pinprick in that torso and the whole thing would collapse", wrote the ferocious Huysmans.

Boldini, who came from Ferrara, settled in Paris from 1872 and became the portrait painter of the Paris smart set. Everything is carefully staged in his canvases. Here, the waved hair, the carriage of the head, the gloves and cane of the Count of Montesquiou, painted in a range of subtle greys, immortalise the man who was considered the arbiter of elegance at the end of the century.

3

2

A friend of Degas, and a private tutor, it was, however, in solemn poses and through the use of sound technique that Léon Bonnat immortalised the celebrities of the Third Republic in scrupulously lifelike portraits that stand out against the solid backgrounds.

4

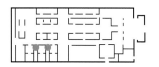

These works can be viewed in rotation on the ground floor, in Rooms 17 and 21, and on the top floor, in Rooms 37, 38 and 40.

The strength of the outline

Before becoming a painter, Daumier was first a cartoonist, a skill which he would never give up. Thus it is that, in addition to his well-known political caricatures, he relentlessly, and in caustic outlines, sketched the quirks of his contemporaries – the middle-classes, doctors and lawyers –, succeeding, in the opinion of Baudelaire, in making a "serious art" of cartoons.

2

1

3

In his numerous Conté crayon drawings, Seurat, completely abandoning the outline, delicately shapes his forms using masses of light and shade which he treats with subtle gradations. This elegant mysterious woman recalls the female contours of his large canvases.

The inscription in Boudin's hand on the back: "Storm effect Sky dark distant impenetrable… heat animals placid", bear witness to the role of preparation that these studies played in working out the canvases, sorts of aide-mémoires on which he recorded postures, colours and notes on the weather conditions.

Between 1879 and 1882, Manet produced a magnificent series of portraits of elegant women. Here, in refined harmonies of white, grey and black, he shows the beautiful lady of Vienna in profile, under a large black hat, as he would do in a second pastel depicting the same model.

4

From 1862, Boudin began to paint seascapes and beach scenes at Trouville and Deauville: it was there that the Imperial Court indulged in the new delights of sea-bathing, soon joined by the polite society of the era. Using horizontal formats that suited the subject matter well, the artist painted from life silhouettes reduced to coloured spots. Working in the open air and striving to produce "a fairly sincere reproduction of the world of my time", he thus paved the way for the Impressionists. This work is one of 5,742 drawings bequeathed to the Musée du Luxembourg by Boudin's heirs.

5

1. LUCIEN LÉVY-DHURMER, *Woman with Medal* or *Mystery*, 1896, pastel and gold highlights, 35 x 54 cm
2. ODILON REDON, *The Madman* or *Madness: Head in a Cap*, around 1877, charcoal, 36.2 x 31.4 cm
3. PAUL CÉZANNE, *Mount Sainte-Victoire*, 1900-1902, water-colour and gouache with graphite, 31.1 x 47.7 cm
4. EDGAR DEGAS, *Bathtub*, 1886, pastel, 60 x 83 cm

These works can be viewed in rotation on the ground floor, in Rooms 17 and 21, and on the top floor, in Rooms 37, 38 and 40.

From reality to the dream

Like Degas, Lévy-Dhurmer was very skilled in using pastels, but from a different viewpoint, since this technique enabled him to evoke mysterious worlds animated with imaginary figures.

For more than thirty years, Redon devoted himself almost solely to drawing, with a marked preference for charcoal. This moving face, the head covered by a cap with small bells on it – like the mad used to wear? – and the eyes full of anguish, remains enigmatic. "The description, by a title given to my drawings, is sometimes too much, so to speak," wrote Redon. "Its title is only justified when it is vague, indeterminate, and alluding, even confusedly, to the ambiguous. My drawings *inspire* and are not defined. The do not lead to anything. Like music, they place us in the ambiguous world of the indeterminate."

From 1890, Cézanne end-lessly painted and drew Mount Sainte-Victoire. A few brushs-trokes of translucent colour are enough, here, to evoke the powerful, immovable nature of this Provençal mountain bathed in light.

3

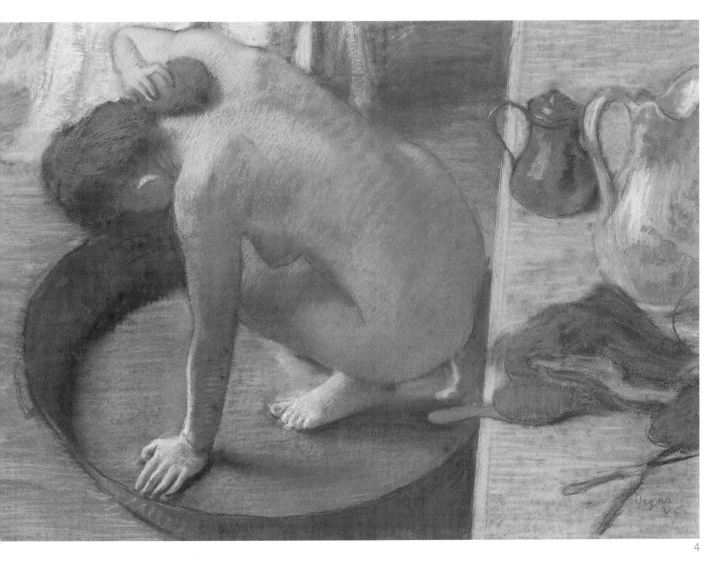

4

Between 1878 and about 1890, Degas executed in pastels a series of nudes getting washed, who seemed to be unconcerned at being observed: "Until now, the nude had always been depicted in poses suggesting an audience, but my women are simple, honest people atten-ding to nothing more than their physical existence. This is one of them: she is washing her feet. It is as if you were looking through the key-hole." The perspective, seen from above, by which the shelf on which the washing items stand seems to be vertical, was inspired by the for-mat of Japanese prints – we know that Degas had hanging over his bed a print portraying women in a bath-house. The technique of using pastels, which he would resort to more and more often as the years went by, enabled him to shape the supple, full bodies in such a way that the subtle nuances of light and shade reproduce the texture of the skin.

1. FÉLIX TOURNACHON, known as NADAR, *Portrait of Baudelaire*, circa 1854, experiment on saline paper, 24 x 17.5 cm
2. CHARLES HUGO, *Victor Hugo on the Rocher des Proscrits in Jersey*, 1853, experiment on saline paper ['papier salé'], 17.4 x 17.5 cm
3. EDWARD MUYBRIDGE, *Jumping an Obstacle*, in *Animal locomotion*, published in 1887, facsimile of a plate in the album
4. AUGUSTE and LOUIS LUMIÈRE, *Place des Cordeliers in Lyon, Tramways*, 1895. Frames

These works are exhibited in rotation on the top floor, in Room 49 (level 4)

Freeze frame

Found amongst Baudelaire's papers, this portrait was executed by Nadar, a friend of the poet. In his *Salon de 1859*, however, the writer had lost his temper at this mechanical process: "… the photographic industry is the refuge of all unsuccessful painters, not gifted enough or too lazy to finish their studies… It is self-evident that the industry, in breaking in on art, becomes its most mortal enemy, and that the confusion of functions prevents any from being properly fulfilled… If it [photography] is allowed to encroach upon the domain of the impalpable and the imaginary, upon everything which is only valid because Man brings to it his soul, then woe betide us!"

Having joined his father in exile in Jersey, Charles Hugo devoted himself to photography. Each of his negatives is carefully staged, as in this portrait of the painter in which the smallness of the figure emphasises still more his isolation.

3

With chronophotography, the "photographic production of sequential images, taken at precisely measured intervals of time", the American Muybridge and the Frenchman Jules Marey succeeded in breaking down movement. It was in this way that Muybridge managed to obtain his first snap-shots of horses and prove, against all expectation, that a galloping or trotting horse has all four feet off the ground.

4

On Saturday, 28th December 1895, the first public showing of "cinematography" organised by the Lumière brothers took place in the basement of the Grand Café in Paris. An apparatus set up at the back of the room ran sixteen still images a second printed on a film against a white screen, and thus produced the illusion of movement. Astounded and enthusiastic, the audience were shown, in this way, *Demolition of a Wall*, *Leaving the Lumière Factory*, *Getting into a Train at La Ciotat Station*, *Hoisted by his own Petard*. Cinema was born, an invention "with no commercial future", as the Lumière brothers' father had described it.

1. CHARLES-GUILLAUME DIEHL (cabinet-maker), JEAN BRANDELY (decorator), EMMANUEL FREMIET (sculptor), *Medallist*, 1867, cedar, walnut, ebony, oak, ivory, bronze and silvered copper, 238 x 151 x 60 cm
2. CHRISTOFLE & Co, *Crater*, around 1870, silvered and partially gilded galvanic copper, 38.6 x 42 x 38.2 cm, belonging to a facsimile collection of the Hildesheim treasure
3. FRANÇOIS-DÉSIRÉ FROMENT-MEURICE, *Dressing-table and accoutrements*, 1847-1851, silver, bronze, oak, copper, iron, enamel niello, gold, precious stones, glass, 80 x 188 x 109 cm (table)

These works are situated on the ground floor, in Rooms 9 and 10.

The period of Eclecticism

This piece of furniture places great emphasis on the sculptures which, depicting the triumph of Merovaeus, deliberately at the time, shows evidence of a some-time narcissistic national consciousness.

In the field of the gold-and silversmith's art, the develop-ment of electroplating – which makes it possible, using electricity, to apply a fine layer of precious metal over objects produced from a common alloy – gave the middle-classes the opportunity of having access to silverware. Even though it continued to make unique items in solid silver, Christofle's at that time underwent tremendous expansion as a result of this new process.

1

3

The number of items making up this washing set – table, mirror, ewer, basin, pair of candelabras and cabinet – is unequalled except by the artists who shared in creating it: a gold – and silversmith, an architect, two sculptors, an ornamentalist and several enamellers. In fact, there is a coming together here of early techniques brought up to date, mixed with stylistic elements of past civilisations, which makes this set a perfect example of the Eclecticism which was rife in France from the reign of Louis-Philippe, and which would endure in the decorative arts throughout the Second Empire. Commissioned at the time of the marriage of the Princess of Parma, granddaughter of Charles X, this unique set was enormously successful at the Great Exhibition in London. In 1836, in *La Confession d'un enfant du siècle*, Alfred de Musset evoked this "curious century" that was the 19th, a "century of borrowings". Can one find a better illustration of these words?

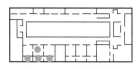

1. LOUIS COMFORT TIFFANY and HENRI DE TOULOUSE-LAUTREC, *At the New Circus, Papa Chrysanthème*, 1895, "American" glass, cabochons, 120 x 85 cm
2. RENÉ LALIQUE, *Neck chain and Dragonfly pendant*, 1903-1905, gold, enamel, gems and aquamarines; pendant: 6.9 x 5.7 x 0.8 cm; chain: 41.5 cm
3. HECTOR GUIMARD, Fonderies de Saint-Dizier, *Central panel for main balcony*, 1905-1907, cast, 81 x 173 cm
4. ALEXANDRE CHARPENTIER (sculptor) and ALEXANDRE BIGOT (ceramist), *Dining-Room*, 1900-1901, acajou-mahogany, oak, poplar, gilded bronze and enamelled clay, 346 x 1,055 x 621 cm

These works are situated on the middle floor, in Rooms 62, 63, 64 and 66.

Faced with Eclecticism,
a "New Art" in Paris

Like ceramics, lights, furniture, carpets and stained glass play an important part in Art Nouveau architecture. It was during a trip to the United States that the Paris merchant Bing discovered the iridescent glassware of the painter turned master glassmaker, Tiffany. On his return to France, Bing asked his friends – Bonnard, Denis, Vallotton, Toulouse-Lautrec – to make several sketches for stained-glass windows.

1

The great jeweller of Art Nouveau, Lalique, designed pieces of jewellery that were remarkable and innovative not only in terms of taking their inspiration from nature – flowers and insects –, but also in terms of the materials he used: precious materials, as well as glass, horn, semi-precious stones, enamels and the like.

2

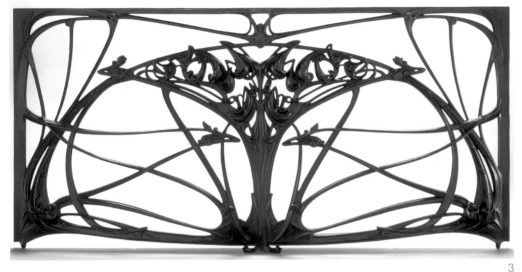

After seeing the private residences built by Horta in Brussels, Guimard threw himself into constructing "castels", strange buildings with sinuous arabesques. He also designed furniture, balconies, jardinières, and entrances to Metro stations, where the motif of stems is a recurring one.

3

4

In the 1890's, a number of artists reacted against the pervading Eclecticism to define a new language dubbed "Art nouveau" in France. From now on, they tried to work together to design projects in which architecture, sculpted scenery, furniture and decorative objects harmonised with one another. This is what Charpentier and Bigot produced on behalf of a banker and developer of the Paris Metro, Adrien Bénard: panelling in light acajou-mahogany sculpted from supple wood, furniture with very simple, undulating lines incorporated into the panelling and items of furniture, some of which are no longer around today.

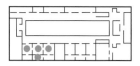

1. ÉMILE GALLÉ, *Hand with Seaweed and Shell-fish*, 1904, cut crystal with inclusions and applications, 33.4 x 13.4 cm
2. LOUIS MAJORELLE and DAUM BROTHERS, *"Nénuphar" lamp*, 1902-1903, pâte-de-verre, gilded bronze, 60.5 x 16.5 cm
3. HENRY VAN DE VELDE, *Writing-desk*, 1898-1899, oak, gilded bronze, copper, leather, 128 x 268 x 122 cm
4. VICTOR HORTA, *Panelling and furniture from the hôtel Aubecq*, 1902-1904, ash, "American" glass, copper, modern fittings
5. LOUIS MAJORELLE, *Bureau "Orchids"*, 1903-1905, acajou-mahogany, tortoiseshell wood, gilded bronze, copper, leather, 95 x 170 x 70 c

These works are situated on the middle floor, in Rooms 61, 63, 64 and 65.

The Nancy school and Art Nouveau in Belgium

Gallé, a glassmaker, and also a ceramist and cabinet-maker, was the central figure of the Nancy school, an association of craftsmen and industrialists from Lorraine who came together from around 1880, enthused by the idea of a total art whose inspiration was to be drawn chiefly from nature. He took over his father's studio, where soon several hundred workers were engaged in mass-producing designs, whilst he continued to create objects only copied a few times. Throughout his life, he sought to turn glass into a sort of stone, creating extraordinary colours and materials using various engraving, inclusion and application techniques, and developing new firing processes.

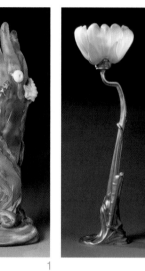

1   2

Like Gallé, Majorelle exercised his art in several areas: he also designed decorative items, such as this lamp manufactured by the Daum brothers.

More a theoretician than Horta and far less "decorative", Van de Velde envisaged ornament not as decoration but as a means of emphasising the structure and functionality of the object. The refined, elegant lines of this office differ from the convoluted and naturalist shapes of a considerable number of Art Nouveau artists and herald a certain simplification in furniture and architecture: based in Berlin, then in Weimar, Van de Velde would be considered as the forerunner of the Bauhaus school.

4

In Brussels, the architect Horta designed several private residences for members of the rich middle-class, such as the industrialist Octave Aubecq, for whom he built an ultra-modern house, a triumph of light and ribbing used as a decorative motif. It is said that Mme Aubecq detested this house and that her children, talking about their parents' house, used to say: "I'm off to Horta's." On Aubecq's death, the house was pulled down and his wife recovered stones and materials.

5

After studying in Paris, Majorelle returned to Nancy to take over the family furniture business. His style was marked by a preference for dark woods and large gilded bronzes which derived their shapes from flora and highlighted the lines of his furniture. A library with the same orchid-motif decoration completes this office.

3

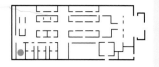

1. CHARLES RENNIE MACINTOSH, *Commode and dressing-table mirror,* from Hous'Hill, Glasgow, 1904, lacquered wood, ebony, mother-of-pearl, glass, silvered brass, 79.8 x 101.6 x 45.7 cm (commode)
2. WILLIAM MORRIS and WILLIAM DE MORGAN, glazed earthenware tile panel, decoration from Membland Hall, 1876-1877, 163 x 90 cm
3. FRANK LLOYD WRIGHT, Linden Glass Company, Chicago, *Pair of leaded glass windows,* around 1908, glass, zinc, 112 x 104 cm

These works are situated in Rooms 26 and 27, accessible via Room 24, on the ground floor.

In England and the United States

In England, the Arts & Crafts movement, appearing around 1850 in reaction to Eclecticism, advised and defended an ideal whose first principles – a return to artisanship and industrial spread – were almost impossible to reconcile. One of its theoreticians, William Morris, founded the firm Morris & Co. in 1861, which was soon making mass-produced objects that very quickly achieved immense success. Wall-paper, hangings, carpets, ceramics and furniture were divided between refined aesthetics, with simple lines, and a taste for decors abounding in rather lavish materials and colours.

The Glasgow school, a Scottish version of Art Nouveau, extended the Arts & Crafts movement in a refined form in which objects deliberately asserted their function through stiff horizontal and vertical lines which emphasised their structure. Macintosh, the most outstanding character in this group, perfectly illustrated this style in which naturalist motifs had almost vanished in favour of abstract decorative elements.

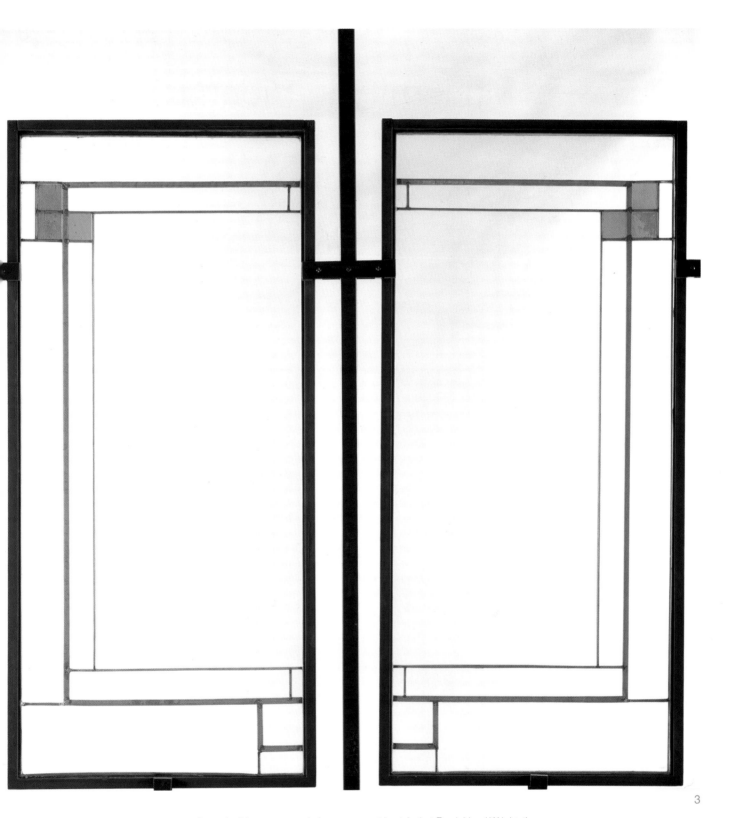

3

It was to this same pared-down, geometric style that Frank Lloyd Wright, the famous Chicago architect came and, influenced by Japanese art, designed houses whose natural materials aimed to integrate them completely into their location. Inside, the space is open and free from partitioning, and it is the furniture which thus takes over the task of breaking up the volumes.

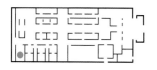

1. FIRME THONET FRÈRES, *Chair no. 4, 51* and *56*, 'frime' created in 1853, dyed bowed beech, cane bottom 90 cm;
    bottom right, JOSEF URBAN, 'Chaine firme', Thonet, around 1905, black varnished beech, dyed leather, brass, 98.5 cm
2. KOLOMAN MOSER, Wiener Werkstätte, *Music Cabinet*, around 1904, oak, gilded wood, metal, silvered metal, glass,
    199.5 x 200.5 x 65.5 cm
3. JOSEF HOFFMANN, JOSEF BERGER, Wiener Werkstätte, *Jardinière*, 1903-1904, silvered metal, 11 x 39.2 x 12.2 cm

These works are situated in Room 27, accessible via Room 24, on the ground floor.

Modernity in Vienna

1

"To maintain our furniture in good condition, please tighten the screws and bolts three or four times a year. Thonet Frères, 15, boulevard Poissonnière. Paris", reads a label inside the band of this chair. Thus it was that, from the end of the 1840's, a French cabinet-maker established in Vienna in 1842, Michael Thonet, in reaction to Eclecticism and Neo-Rococo, devised simple, solid furniture that was comfortable and fine-looking, intended for hotels, cafés and restaurants, and produced by the process in which wood is curved using steam. Here, quality attempted to go hand in hand with industrial production.

his "Art Nouveau" was quite different to that
hich was then current in France and
elgium: curves had given way to straight
es and a style both pared-down and refi-
ed, which is well represented by this *Music
abinet*. It was not through these unique
eces reserved for a well-off clientele that
is aesthetic quality would be spread, howe-
er: these artists very soon provided designs
r furniture, chinaware and glassware for fac-
ries whose mass-produced items would,
efore long, pass on the new ideas to the
eneral public.

2

3

At the very beginning of the 20th century in Vienna,
the artists of the Sezession – Otto Wagner, Koloman
Moser or Josef Hoffmann – founded the Wiener
Werkstätte, the Viennese Studio, a sort of guild aimed
at regenerating the decorative arts. Their principles
were clear: "We start with the object's function, its
handiness is our first concern. Our strength lies in
the proper treatment of the material. The work of the
craftsman must be assessed by the same yardstick
as that of the painter and sculptor", they stated in their
Work schedule published in 1905.

Achevé d'imprimer le 20 octobre 2005
par les Presses de Bretagne
Dépôt légal : novembre 2005